W9-AFZ-363

NO MAN CAN HINDER ME

The **JOURNEY** *from* **SLAVERY** *to* **EMANCIPATION** *through* **SONG**

V E L M A   M A I A   T H O M A S

Crown Publishers
New York

ENERGY OF MOVEMENT (TOP)
Traditional African nations such as the mighty Zulu empire used dance to prepare themselves for the whirl of battle.

REJOICING (BELOW)
Native Kenyans had a variety of carefully choreographed dances to celebrate important events in the community. The images below and on the opposite page are from festivities circa 1940.

Remember Me: S O N G S *of* A F R I C A

MUSIC HAS LONG BEEN a part of my people's culture and tradition. African villages were filled with drumming, the sounds of horns, songs and dance. Music unified the people. In music they rejoiced, recounted their shared history, and announced the good news and the bad. Said the once enslaved African Olaudah Equiano of his people, "We are almost a nation of dancers, musicians, and poets. Thus every great event, such as triumphant return from battle, or other cause of public rejoicing is celebrated in public dance which are accompanied with song and music."[1] The African and the music were one.

Early European travelers wrote of the African's love of music. Songs chronicled life's events. The African sang of courtship and marriage, at the birth of a child, to announce a youth's rites of passage into adulthood. There were songs of work, for fishing, hunting, planting, and harvesting. Songs were a part of burial rituals—music was there at wakes and funerals. A thief was called out, a beautiful woman admired, the king praised in chants and song. At every turn, at every gathering, the African had a song.

My ancestors enjoyed complex rhythms, with overlapping beats and tempos. Rhythm was syncopated; it ebbed and flowed with precision. So different was the African's sense of timing that an Englishman studying African music was compelled to write: "African rhythm is so complicated that it is exceedingly difficult for a European to analyze it…any piece of European music has at any one moment one rhythm in common, a piece of African music always has two or three sometimes as many as four. From this point of view European music is childishly simple."[2]

The dancer, too, lent his talent. The African swayed, stamped his feet, moved her torso, or leaped in the air. Village dancers formed a circle, chanting and singing to their ancestors. No one stood still and sang. For the African, such was impossible. One enjoyed music with his entire body. White visitors were mesmerized by my people's agility. An Englishman among the Ibo of Nigeria conceded, "The twisting, turning, contortions and springing movement executed in perfect time, are wonderful to behold....For these set dances...the physical strength required is tremendous. The body movements are extremely difficult and would probably kill a European."[3]

While music was entertaining and educational, it was also sacred and healing. Music was a part of every ritual. Dance, music, and song raised the energy of the participants. Participants heard, saw, and experienced things that the rational mind could not. Man's defenses came down when the songs went up. The Kung people of the Kalahari Desert in South Africa experienced the power of receiving a *num* song from God. According to the Kung, it is the *num*, the most powerful energy force in creation, that heals.

Around a fire, in healing rituals that begin at dusk and could last well into dawn, the Kung dance and sing. Men and women enter heightened states of consciousness, aided by the num songs, by rhythmic dancing. Should one faint away, overcome by the power of the spirit, another moves in to take his or her place—the circle remains unbroken. Participants go into a trance. The singers, dancers, and healers have tapped into the power of the universe. The num has reached its boiling point, *kia*. In that moment, those afflicted physically, emotionally, and spiritually are healed.

It was this knowledge of the power of music, of ritual, of song and dance that Africans gave to the world. Aboard the slave ship, on the auction block, in the fields, their music survived. It was passed down through generations, traveling across space and time. Just as the Zulu of South Africa sang while they worked, so too did the enslaved Africans in America. As women sang threshing rice in a village in Liberia, so too did they sing as they performed the same task on the Sea Islands of coastal Georgia. As African men and women formed a sacred circle in their rituals, so too did they in the ring shouts on plantations. Only the language was different; the feeling, the power, and the emotion were the same.

The songs my people sang were theirs—the music of Africans born in America. They were nurtured by generations of Africans who had sung them before. The call of the drum, the rhythm of the dance, the charm and soothing of the songs were the same in America as in Africa. It was this music that sustained, encouraged, and empowered them. It was this music that took them home, home to Africa where rituals, power, joy, and life began.

The Middle Passage:

SONGS THAT CARRIED US OVER

EXCESS BAGGAGE (TOP)
*Slaves that were seriously
ill or wounded were thrown
overboard to die.*

FOR SALE (BELOW)
*Handbills, like this example from
1769, advertised slave auctions
in large American coastal cities,
where ships pulled into port
with their human cargo.*

THE SONGS OF MY PEOPLE filled the slave vessels. Those shackled below the deck sang songs of sorrow, of longing for home, of petition to their God for strength, and yes, songs welcoming death. Upon realizing that they could not escape, that they had no weapons strong enough to defeat the enslaver, many Africans chose death. Wrote Dr. Isaac Wilson, a surgeon aboard the slave ship *Elizabeth*, "Even in the act of chastisement, I have seen them look up at me with a smile, and in their own language, say 'presently we shall be no more.' " [4]

The horror of the capture and the Middle Passage — the journey from Africa to slavery in a foreign land — remained vivid in captives' minds. Africans remembered small vessels coming to the shore, enticing them with gifts, red cloth, and beads onto beckoning ships that lay waiting at sea. Charlie Grant of Marion, South Carolina, a former slave, told: "Dey fooled dem to come or I calls it foolin' dem. De peoples go to Africa en when dey go to dock, dey blow whistles en de peoples come from all over de country to see what it was. Dey fool dem on de vessel en give dem somethin' to eat. Shut dem up en don't let dem get out." [5]

Once aboard the ships, my people were gripped with fear. Without warning, for reasons they could not understand, they were bound, branded, whipped, and herded into the hold of the ship. Tales of the horror of the Middle Passage were passed by Africans from generation to generation. "Uncle Ephraim" remembered his grandfather's account of being aboard a slave ship in the middle of a storm. The elder African remembered the starvation, death, and despair of those in chains: "Waves beatin' 'gainst de boat, 'cause it's stormy. No big steamships lak dey got terday.... Grandfadder say dey got rows o' cells lak a jailhouse. Dey puts de men on one side de boat, an' de women on de uddah…"

Ephraim revealed how the Africans comforted themselves and each other: "Den dey sings. One sings. One sings, an' de res' hum lak. What de sing? Nobody don' know. It's not ouu'ah words. De sing language what dey learn in Africa when dey was free." [6]

Enslavers wrote similar accounts of the melancholy tunes of the Africans. Wrote Dr. Claxton after his voyage aboard the slave vessel *The Young Hero:* "They sing, but not for their amusement. To stave off melancholy that often led to revolt or suicide, the captain ordered them to sing, and they sang songs of sorrow. Their sickness, fear of being beaten, their hunger, and the memory of their country, are the usual subjects."[7] In his *Account of the Slave Trade*, ship surgeon Alexander Falconbridge recorded the same. "Their music, upon these occasions, consists of a drum. The poor wretches are frequently compelled to sing also; but when they do so, their songs are generally, as may naturally be expected, melancholy lamentations of their exile from their native land. Such were the sad origins of the Negro rhythms which have since conquered the Western world."[8]

But my people's songs were not the only haunting voices aboard the ships. Captains and crew, tired of the voyage, afraid of insurrection, victims of the same diseases that felled the blacks, found the Middle Passage sickening, the Slave Coast deadly. Africa would have her revenge. On those who stole her children she inflicted yellow fever, dengue, blackwater fever, malaria, hookworm, dysentery, and more. In the eyes of the enslaver, Africa became "the white man's grave." Eighteenth-century abolitionist Thomas Clarkston conducted several studies of the mortality of crews aboard slave ships. His study of nine vessels that sailed between 1766 and 1780 revealed 11 percent of the 203-member crews perished compared to 6.5 percent of the 2,362 slaves. Aboard the slave vessel *Molly*, 7 of 13 crew members died, and approximately 50 of the 105 enslaved. On the *Surrey*, 4 of 25 seamen lost their lives, while 10 of the 225 Africans died.[9] So deadly became the voyages that the crews were heard to sing, "Beware and take care, Of the Bight of Benin; For one that comes out, There are forty go in."

Still the ships came. Slavers reconciled their actions, turning a deaf ear to the dirges of Africans and their own crews. It would take Captain John Newton, a slave trader who later became an abolitionist and Anglican priest, more than twenty years to see the wretchedness of his ways. Even after his religious conversion, he continued to trade in flesh. While waiting on the coast for slaves to bring to America, Newton penned "How Sweet the Name of Jesus": "How sweet the name of Jesus sounds in a believer's ear! It soothes his sorrows, heals his wounds, and drives away his fear." Surely my people listened intently to the songs of the enslaver, then must have watched in wonder as he conducted what appeared to be religious services aboard the ship. They stood in horror as Captain Newton applied the thumbscrews to one of his own, accused of plotting a mutiny. When Newton left the slaving business, he confessed to being a sinner, saved only by merciful God. The hymn he wrote, "Amazing Grace," was his testimony of his own wretchedness and salvation.

Such were the songs that went out across the Atlantic. Songs in African languages now forgotten, hymns still sung in Protestant churches. Perhaps in West Africa, black mothers still wail for children taken away on slave ships long ago. The ancient songs have not died; they are only awaiting a reply.

"KUM BA YA"

Although today a popular campfire song, "Kum Ba Ya" is a Negro spiritual that appeals to God for comfort in a hostile land. Some believe that "kum ba ya" is a mispronunciation of "come by here," spoken by Africans struggling with a strange new language. Others believe the words may be a variation of "Kum baba yana," which appears in several songs sung by Africans who remembered their native tongue. A plaintive song, "Kum Ba Ya" attests to my people's faith in a God who hears the cries of His people and who, when petitioned, responds.

Kum Ba Ya, My Lord
Kum Ba Ya
Kum Ba Ya, My Lord
Kum Ba Ya
Kum Ba Ya, My Lord
  (oh Lord)
Kum Ba Ya
Oh Lord, Kum Ba Ya

Someone's praying, Lord
  (Hear our prayer, Lord)
Kum Ba Ya
Someone's praying, Lord
Kum Ba Ya
Someone's praying, Lord
  (oh Lord)
Kum Ba Ya
Oh Lord, Kum Ba Ya

Lord, How Come Me Here?

HOLDING on to SONGS of OUR AFRICAN PAST

DANCING THE JUBA (TOP)

The Juba was a popular dance that showed off the performer's skills in dancing, singing, and rhythm.

JACK, GUINEA DRIVER (BELOW)

This daguerreotype of an enslaved African from Guinea, West Africa, was taken as part of a study of African morphological types by J.T. Zealy in 1850. Slaveholders did not give Jack a last name, but he was an overseer of other slaves, hence the designation "Driver."

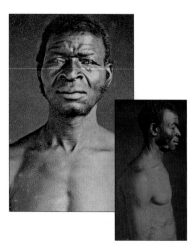

FOR THE NEW AFRICAN arrival, America must have been a lonely world. Those who survived the Middle Passage now had to withstand the trauma and torture—physical and psychological—of chattel slavery. My people held on to as much of Africa as they could, learning to adapt to European culture in order to survive. Slaveholders thrust upon them new names, new religion, new family structure, new values. They stripped away anything African—the family, the language, the rituals. No wonder, with pain in their hearts, my people sang, "Lord, how come me here? I wish I never was born.… Ain't no freedom here, Lord, I wish I never was born."

Whites were always wary when my people got together. The singing, the beating of the drum seemed to bring the enslaved to a religious frenzy, giving them ideas of Africa and power and freedom. Gabriel Prosser in 1800, Demark Vesey in 1822, and Nat Turner in 1831 proved that the planters' fears of gathered blacks were not always ill founded. Quoting from the Bible, calling on their African ancestors, meeting in secret and compelling free blacks and slaves to rise, these men plotted three slave insurrections—put down only by a violent white reprisal.

A hymn such as this raised the whites' suspicion: "Some friends has gone before me, I must try to go and meet them, Glory Hallelujah. A few more risings and the setting of the sun, Ere the winter will be over, Glory Hallelujah. There's a better day a-coming, There's a better day a-coming, Oh, Glory Hallelujah."

After Nat Turner's rebellion, slaveholders and lawmakers clamped down on slave gatherings. They made it illegal for slaves to assemble without permission; confiscated the drum and punished those beating it in secret; forbade "Negro church meetings" unless there was a white person present. Planters forbade Africans to practice their indigenous religions. Slaveholders taught their slaves a Christianity that told them to be docile and obedient to their masters—a message that did not bode well with many of my people.

Those who accepted Christianity did so under their own terms and in their own ways. My people may have sat passively in services held by whites, but in their own services—secret meetings held in the fields—their worship took on a heartfelt expression. There, outside the view of the master, they sang, exhorted, kept alive the ring shout that made their worship distinctly African. They enjoyed the ring shout, a gathering of people in a circle to concentrate and invoke energy and power. "Shouters" would form a circle, moving counterclockwise in a unified motion. They moved their feet back and forth in a shuffle, feet would never cross, never leave the floor. Timekeepers stood to the side, clapping their hands or stamping their feet. The worshippers'—participants and supporters—songs were the "call and response," with song leader and congregation "basers" who sang in deep tones, alternating as they sang.

Singers would begin, timekeepers would use heavy staffs to pound a steady beat. Supporters would clap a complementary faster rhythm. The tempo might increase as the fervor intensified, peaked, and finally subsided. According to slaves and their descendants, shouts could last from night until the morning hours.

{LEADER WOULD "CALL"}

"In that morning, true believer"

{CONGREGATION WOULD RESPOND}

"In that morning"

"We will sit aside Jesus,"

"In that morning"

"If you should go 'fore I go,"

"In that morning"

"You will sit aside Jesus."

"In that morning"

"True believers, where your tickets?"

"In that morning"

"Master Jesus got your tickets."

"In that morning"

My people kept their African traditions alive in their funerals and burial rites. In America, as in Africa, my people sat up all night with the deceased, praying and protecting the spirit. They sang as they carried the body to the burial place, sprinkled the site with broken glass or pottery, or placed in the grave a bottle of rum or food for the deceased to take with him on his journey home. "Moonlight—Starlight, O-o-h Moonlight, Believer what's the matter, John lay the body down, John lay the body down. John lay the body to the tomb, O-o-h let me go, John lay the body to the tomb, John lay the body down." And in their ecstasy of knowing the departed was going to a better place where they could rest and wouldn't be dressed in rags anymore, you could hear my people rejoice. "I got shoes, you got shoes, all God's chillen got shoes, when I git to Heaben, I'm a-goin' to put on my shoes, an' walk all over God's Heaben."

This spiritual journey was only one trip my people took. They also talked about going back home—home to Africa. Some were successful in returning. In 1815, 38 free blacks sailed with Paul Cuffe, a black sea captain who returned to Sierra Leone, West Africa. Between 1817 and 1850 more than 12,000 free blacks and manumitted slaves were transported to West Africa by the American Colonization Society. *The African Repository*, the official newspaper of the American Colonization Society, recorded: "a conservative slave told his Quaker benefactor that he wanted to 'cross over' to Africa, the home of his camp meeting. Accordingly the slave sang, 'Deep River, my home is over Jordan, Deep River, Lord, I want to cross over into camp ground.'" [10]

Some who wanted to go could not, yet they held to the memory of Africa. Despite the Middle Passage, despite their adaptation to a new life and new culture, Africa would remain a part of them. It was a memory, a ritual, a song, or a dance that could not, would not, die.

When the Hammer Rings:

SONGS of WORK

FAMILY TIME (TOP)
Cotton was king on Southern plantations. During peak harvest times, entire slave families worked in the fields together.

THE DAILY GRIND (BELOW)
Agriculture drove the economy of the South. The work was backbreaking and lasted from sunup until sundown.

WORK SONGS HAVE ALWAYS filled the air when my people labored. Songs took one's mind off the grueling task at hand. They built camaraderie, reinforced what one felt—soon this hard, sweatin', dirty job would be done. When asked why the men sang while they worked, a black Alabama track liner replied, "Singing just naturally makes the work go easier. If you didn't have singing you wouldn't get hardly anything out of these men." [11]

If one had to work all one's life, if there was no relief from the toil, one could make the tasks more bearable with a song. "Don't mind working from sun to sun, Iffen you give me my dinner—When the dinner time comes!" My people may have sung this tune in jest, but when the overseer was a safe distance away, there rose a different song. "If I live, Sangaree, See nex' fall, Sangaree, Ain't gon' t' plant, Sangaree, No cotton at all."

The sound of my people's songs was comforting to slaveholders' ears, their melodies soothing, their voices breaking the stillness of the day. Georgia Bryan Conrad remarked of the slaves on her father's plantation, "In the fields carrying their burdens rowing or feeding the mill with rice, the Negroes were always singing...As I recall those days, it is ever with a sound of melody in my ears." [12] Although their songs may have been pleasing to slave owners, pleasure was hardly the effect for the slaves themselves. Often songs masked my people's true feelings. They sang not because they were happy, but because the songs provided the strength to carry on. "Sometimes I'm up, sometimes I'm down, In dat ole fiel', But still my soul is heaven boun', In dat ole fiel'."

My people worked constantly, rising in the morning at the sound of the horn, toiling until dusk—or dark or midnight if the moon was bright. Hands were expected to pick at least 100 pounds of cotton each day; sure punishment awaited if they fell short of their quota. James Walton, a former slave, looked back and remembered, "Us slaves had to do a certain amount of tasks a day. Even us kids had to pick a hunnert and fifty pound of cotton a day, or get a whoppin'." [13] If nature

worked against them, if the cotton rotted on the stalks, some pickers put their woes to song. "Way down in the bottom — wah the cotton boll's rotten. Won't get my hundrud all day." Others declared they'd leave the bad stalk and move on to the next. Their song told others, "Befo'e I'll be beated — befo'e I'll be cheated, I'll leave five finguhs in the boll." (Some varieties of cotton had only three or four leaves, or fingers, that held the fibers; others had five.)

Slaves in the rice fields sang as they planted and harvested grain. Fields had to be prepared in the winter. Slaves turned and hoed the ground, cleaned and repaired canals and ditches. They planted in the spring, flooded the fields in the summer. In late summer they harvested the grain, hacking at rice stalks with sickles. My people labored in such unhealthy conditions, a visitor on the Sea Island Coast remarked: "The labor required for the cultivation is fit only for slaves, and I think the hardest work I have seen them engaged in." [14]

Still the work had to be done. As they thrashed, stamped, and pounded the grain, my people sang in a rhythmic chant: "I gwine t' beat dis rice, Gwine t' beat 'um so, Gwine t' beat 'um until the hu'ks come off, Ah hanh hanh, Ah hanh hanh. Gwine t' cook dis rice when I get through, Gwine t' cook 'um so, Ah hanh hanh, Ah hanh hanh."

Slaves, with their masters' permission, and free blacks who were skilled could escape the field-work, though not the inequities of working for another, and accept paying jobs. Carpenters, livery-men, brick masons, and other such workers may have been allowed to "hire out" themselves, but it was not guaranteed they would get their just pay. After doing the work, after taking a man at his word, many of my people were handed excuses instead of a dollar, were sent away empty-handed. With growing frustration and little or no recourse, black workers sang of being done wrong. "Pay me, Oh pay me, Pay me my money down, Pay me or go to jail, Pay me my money down. Think I hear my captain say, pay me my money down, T'morrow is my sailin' day, Pay me my money down…. You owe me, pay me, Pay me my money down. Pay me or go to jail, Pay me my money down."

Work and song blended as oarsmen rowed their masters to town or plantation, keeping time with their oars. "Black diamonds are her bright, black eyes, Her teeth and lilies are alike, Sing, fellows, for my true love, And the water with long oar strike."

Slave children remembered hearing their mothers sing as they worked in the fields or the big house. Black women sang while they cooked, rocked babies, cleaned, and mended. Mildred Carter remembered a song sung while spinning thread to make cloth. According to her mother, women would spin the yarn in pairs. One would thread the needle while the other would wind the ball. They would pat their feet and sing, "Wind de ball, wind de ball, don't care how you wind de ball, Wind de ball, lady wind de ball, Ding, ding, ding — wind de ball."

Perhaps the most festive of work songs was sung during corn-husking season. Masters turned the event into big fellowships, with plenty of food, drink, and work. A former Georgia slave remembered: "In corn shucking time, no padderrollers would ever bother you. We would have a big time at corn shucking. They would call up the crowd and line the men up and give them a drink…I was a corn general—would stand out high above everybody, giving out corn songs and throw down corn to them. There would be two sides of them, one side trying to outshuck the other. Such times we had." [15]

Songsters made up ditties on the spot: "Pull de hus, bread de ear, Whoa, I's got de red hear here." As the night and festivities wore on, my people may have added satires: "Massa in the great house, counting out his money, Oh, shuck that corn and throw it in the barn. Mistis in the parlor, eating bread and honey, Oh, shuck that corn and throw it in the barn."

Some might say you haven't heard work songs until you've heard the songs of group labor—the men who cleared fields, laid railroad track, loaded steamships, rolled logs, and chopped trees. Rachel Cruz remembers hearing slaves sing as they cleared the woods for the coming railroad: "They be lined up to a tree, an' dey sing dis song to make de blows…when de sing 'Talk (to de wood)' de all chop together, an' perty soon de git de tree ready to fall an' dey yell 'Hi' and…all scramble out de way quick 'cause you can't never tell what way a pine tree gonna fall." [16]

The lead singer in the gang work party played a most important part. It was by his pace that the work got done. He sang out when to lift and when to "lay it down." He called out "how high" and "which way to go." He would slow the pace, pick it up, call for water, shake it up with a line or two about a pretty girl. Their songs called out the task, their beat held the men to a harmonious flow. With the aid of song, black men laid the tracks. "All I hate about linin' track, This old bars' 'bout to break my back! Big boy, can't you line 'em? Oh boy, can't you line 'em? Oh boy, can't you line 'em? Here we go line them track."

When the work called for men to pull together, song leader and crew developed a pattern. The leader would signal the beginning of the task, the men would indicate when ready. He-ho songs such as this could be heard: "Joe pick 'em up—he heavy, pick 'em up, Joe he heavy, pick 'em up."

Another supervising a big job might call out every task in the words of his song. "Hey—slip slide him—a slip—slide him. Ev'rybody bow down an' put yo' han's to it. Come an' go wid me—come an' go wid me. Heavy—heavy—heavy—hank—back. All right—all right. Draw—back-a draw—back."

Sometimes words could not adequately express the heaviness and the loneliness of laboring for another. When those times came, my people simply let out a "holler"— a piercing, melodious call to one across the field. It was a way of getting relief, of warning that the overseer was near. It was a way of affirming, "I'm still here." An Alabama woman whose father had been a slave shared what she knew.

Her father would raise his voice, "Oo, Who hoo-oo who-hoo," and from a distance, echoing the melody, a comrade would answer, "Yeh-ee-ee, yeh-hee, Yeh-ee-ee, yeh, hee!" [17] Perhaps in early days the calls were African dialects, but as time passed

and memories of Africa faded, the field hollers became wordless tunes.

Despite the singing, there was little true joy in my people's work songs. If they sang, it was to *make* themselves happy, not because they *were* happy. Even when they pulled together, even when their voices filled the air or strokes kept time with the song, my people longed to work for themselves. After they serenaded planters sailing along the river, after they joked and laughed at corn-shucking time, after they worked in synchronized motions laying tracks for the trains, my people often sang the truth of their situation with this song: "We raise de wheat, dey gib us de corn, We bake de bread, dey gib us de cruss, We sif de meal, dey gib us de huss, We peal de meat, dey gib us the skin; And dat's de way dey takes us in."

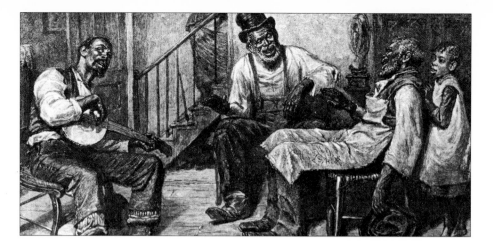

There Must Be a God Somewhere:

The BIRTH of SPIRITUALS

COMMON BOND (TOP)
Carried from one generation to the next, spirituals embodied the hopes and fears of young and old alike.

MIGHTY HYMNS (BELOW)
The undeniable urge to join in with rhythmic clapping, stomping, and dancing were part of the power of spirituals.

SPIRITUALS CAME FROM deep within. They were the moans of the oppressed, the hopes of the slave, the songs of those cruelly mistreated. They were sorrow songs and hope jubilees, religious songs and coded messages of freedom. They had no single author. No one can date them, number them, or name them all. Yet from under the oppression of slavery there arose a song, African in rhythm, scale, and pattern, English in language, Christian in belief.

For more than 100 years, historians and musicologists have argued the origin of spirituals. Some say spirituals are mere imitations of English or even Irish melodies slaves heard their masters sing. Others say they were snatches of Protestant hymns, lines mixed, words mispronounced. Those who sang them knew spirituals were theirs. The words sprang forth from the soul, the melody emerged from life as they lived it. Booker T. Washington, a slave who rose to become the founder of the Tuskegee Institute, explained how he believed spirituals began: "There is in the plantation songs a pathos and a beauty that appeals to a wide range of tastes, and their harmony makes abiding impression upon persons of highest culture. The music of these songs goes to the heart because it comes from the heart." [18] However they came about, few would disagree that spirituals, once heard, could never be forgotten. Their beauty, their longing, their lyrics, and their drones express a human condition and faith as few songs can.

The spirituals captured the essence of Christianity. Wrote John Wesley Work, "In all his [the Negro's] songs there is neither trace nor hint of hatred or revenge…. Doubtless the essence of the Negro character…gave birth to the expression, 'no man can drag me so low as to make me hate him'…. Such a development of race character shows plainly divine intention. The world needs to know that love is stronger than hatred." [19]

Spirituals told of trials and tribulations and the singer's belief in a better day. When one sang spirituals, all present felt the believer's cause. Spirituals were accompanied by motions, clapping, old Car'line! Dis darky fell in love wid a han'some yaller Dinah. Higho-higho-higho." Courting songs were sung to one's beloved, but when a man wanted to make his intentions known, he might joyously sing the songs aloud. "All I want in dis creation, Is pretty little wife and big plantation," or he may rhyme, "Who's been here since I've been gone? Pretty little gal wid a josey on…Never see de like since I was born, Here comes a little gal wid a josey on." No doubt when the young men got together to brag or speak of the women of their choice, you could hear them boast: "You loves yo' gal? Well, I loves mine. Yo' gal hain't common? Well, my gal's fine. I loves my gal, She hain't no goose — Blacker 'an blackberries, Sweeter 'an juice."

Enslaved Africans referred to their loved ones in endearing terms: darling, pretty little girl, honey, and sugar lump. And love was as wide as the sky, as deep as the ocean, or as free as a bird. Lovers often promised each other a beautiful, safe, idyllic world, one quite the opposite of the life they lived under slavery. "Rose's red, vi'let blue. Sugar is sweet but not lak you…De ocean's deep, de sky is blue; Sugar is sweet, an' so is you." They told of a love that would stand the test of time, never knowing when sale would part them, never knowing how long time would be on their side. In stolen hours, perhaps lovers cooed: "De ocean waves an' de sky gits pale, But my love are true, an' it never fails."

They spiced their love with whimsical rhymes. One expressed his love: "I loves coffee, an' I loves tea. I axes you Vinie does you love me? My day's study's Vinie, an' my midnight dreams, My apples, my peaches, my tunnups an' greens." Another told, "Oh, I wish I wus an apple, An' my Sallie was anudder. What a pretty match we'd be, Hanging on a tree togedder!"

Just as there was love, there were heartbreaks, sometimes because the affection was not returned, sometimes because loved ones had to be left behind. A disappointed lover perhaps sang forlornly, "She hug me, an' she kiss me. O Heaben! De touch o' her han'! She said I wus de puttiest thing in de shape o' mortal man. I told her that I love her, Dat my love wus bed-cord strong; Den I axed her w'en she'd have me, An' she jes say 'Go 'Long.' "

One whose love was sold sang with sadness, "Look down dat lonesome road! Look down! De way are dark and col'. Dey makes me weep, dey makes me mourn; All 'cause my love are sol'. O don't you see dat turkle dove, What mourns from vine to vine? She mourns lak I moans fer my love, Lef' many a mile behin'."

If my people appealed, if the slaveholder agreed, slaves could be "married." For most slaves, there was no ceremony; they simply lived together as man and wife. These marriages were special, even though my people knew the slaveholder could dissolve the union at his discretion. My people sought approval from a respected elder of the slave community, who would ask the couple to pray about it and be sure, because marriage was sacred in the eyes of God. Matthew Jarreet recalled, "Arter two days, Mose an' I went back an' say we done thought 'bout it an' still want to git married. Den [Ant Sue] called all de slaves arter tasks to pray

FORTUNATE FEW
Some slave couples were lucky enough to stay together well into old age.

PAINFUL GOODBYE
A slave father is sold away from his family.

occupied, to enchant them with games or song. At times when just singing would not do, mother or caretaker bounced a child on her knee, singing a lively tune. "Mama's little baby loves short'nin', short'nin', Mama's little baby loves short'nin' bread."

Mothers lulled children to sleep with promises of a father's return, even angels to watch over and protect them. "Daddy's comin' home my dahlin', hear him a-whistlin' low; Leave po' daddy jis' one kiss, honey, fo' you go; Den close dem eyes, my honey, deah, dem brown eyes tenduh bright, For God an' angels, mammy's luv, will watch till mawnin' light, Den sleep, my honey, baby dahlin', sleep."

When interviewed as an adult, John Finnely remembered a lullaby from his childhood. "I tell you one singin' but I can't sing it. 'De moonlight, a shinin' star, De big owl hootin' in de tree, O, bye, my baby, ain't you gwineter sleep, A-rockin' on my knee?'"[24]

Although lullabies promised hope, slave mothers knew well that children, like all others enslaved, "belonged" to the master. The auction block could separate children from their mothers, despite a mother's plea. Perhaps at night, failing to mask her fears, a mother sang, "If I rock this baby to sleep, Go to sleep, little baby, Someday he will remember me, Go to sleep, little baby."

Even children who had few or no material items played and had fun. Slave children used their imaginations, made their own toys. They played Bob-a Needle, where children held an object in their hands and secretly passed it to others in the game until the one who was "it" discovered who had the item. When the playmates sang, "Bob-a needle is running," the object was passed around. When they sang, "Bob-a needle ain't a-running," it was in someone's hands. The child who was "it" could then guess who held the item and called out, "You got bob-a."

Girls fashioned dolls out of corncobs, stitched string atop for the doll's hair. Boys made marbles out of sun-baked clay. Pine needles were laced together to build playhouses. Children played house and hide-and-seek, climbed trees, swam, held jumping contests and foot races. For poor children, joy could be found in the little things in life—in games, in nature, in music, in song.

Folklore and fables enchanted slave children's lives. Tales of wily Bruh [Brother] Rabbit outwitting the powerful yet less intelligent Mr. Wolf abound in early African-American fables. Storytellers addressed the animals as "Mister" or "Brother" and brought them to life in song. Rabbits could talk, spiders played tricks, and rhinoceroses, hyenas, and monkeys walked onto Noah's ark. In song, children asked Mr. Rabbit about physical attributes. "Mr. Rabbit, Mr. Rabbit, Your ears are mighty long." To which Mr. Rabbit answered, "Yes, kind sir, they're put on wrong! Every little soul must shine, shine, shine, Every little soul must shine, shine, shine!"

Children complimented animals on their natural beauty and differences. "Fox he got a bushy tail, Raccoon tail am bare, Rabbit got no tail at all, Jes' a leetle bit a bunch er hair." They sang of animals speaking to one other. "Red bird settin' up in de 'simmon tree, Possum settin' on the ground; Sparrow come along un' say, Shake dem 'simmons down."

Perhaps the most popular form of entertainment for children were ring dances. Young people formed a circle and made up games and rhymes played in a ring. In the African tradition, ring games included music, dance, movement, and song. One didn't just sing a song, one acted it out. Lydia Parrish observed of black children on the Sea Islands of Georgia: "They are more melodious than the game songs of the whites; they employ an amusing variety of dance steps, possess a contagious rhythm, and make use of vigorous hand clapping, which is utterly unlike anything European."[25]

So when black children sang "Little Sally Walker," they added movement and words that made them very African. Children formed a circle with one player, "Sally," in the middle. To choose who would be next in the middle, the children of the circle would sing to the child in the center to put her hands on her hips and "shake it to the east, shake it to the west, shake it to the one that you love the best."

Through song, children learned to count. "Once der wus a liddle boy dat couldn' count one. Dey pitched him in a fedder bed; 'e thought it was big fun. Once der wus a liddle boy dat couldn' count two, Dey pitched him in a fedder bed; 'e thought 'e 'us gwine through."

Children made up songs that would teach the parts of their bodies. On the Georgia Sea Islands, children sang and placed their hands on the parts — from head to toe as the song leader called them out. "Pain in the head — Shout — Shout, Shout, Josephine — Shout. Pain in the back — Shout — Shout, Shout, Josephine — Shout."

With hand clapping, leg slapping, and polyrhythms, slave children made their play songs truly African. The best performers could combine song with clapping, allowing them to keep the beat. In "Ham Bone, Ham Bone," singers kept time between each of the lines by patting their hands, thighs (the "ham bone"), and chest in a fast slapping manner. "Ham Bone, Ham Bone, where's you been? All around the world an' back again. Ham Bone, Ham Bone, what'd you do? I got a chance an' I fairly flew."

For most, celebrations were seasonal — Easter, Christmas, and harvest. Julia Frazer of Virginia remembered, "They had parties on Holidays…. On dem days we would play ring plays, jump rope an' dance Juba."[26] "Juba" was a favorite jig, allowing performers to show their dancing, rhythm, and singing skills. Between each line of the song, participants kept time, slapping one knee then the other. "Juba dis and Juba dat, An' Juba killed yalla cat, An' get over double-trouble Juba!" When they sang, "Now Juba," the last words of the song, the singer would jump up and do some fancy footwork to the delight of himself and onlookers.

As they grew older, youth played kissing games. In this game, one of the girls pretended to be asleep while one of the boys circled around her, singing, "Here we go round the strawberry bush, This cold and frosty morning. She wants a young gentleman to wake her up, This cold and frosty morning." A kiss was given, the sleeper awakened, and the game continued with another in the middle.[27]

For many of my people, childhood games had a time and place. Work came first. As the years of slave labor surpassed the carefree years of play, many slaves remembered less of the fun time, more of the labor. Booker T. Washington stated that until he looked back on his life, it never occurred to him that he had had little leisure time as a child. He believed he would have been a "more useful man, had there been more time for sports during my childhood."[28] Despite the rigors of slavery, most black children found time for laughter. They would teach games and songs to their playmates, sing lullabies to their own babies. Where there were children, where there was love, there would be lullabies, laughter, ring games, and songs.

TIME TO PLAY (BELOW)
Three slave children rest from their labors, circa 1860.

24

"HAM BONE, HAM BONE"

Young men preferred songs and games that showed off their ability to keep rhythm or keep up a clever step. In "Ham Bone, Ham Bone," making the slapping sound with one's hands hitting against the body was as important as singing the words.

Aw Ham Bone, Ham Bone, where's you been?
All around the world an' back again.
Ham Bone, Ham Bone, what'd you do?

I got a chance an' I fairly flew.
Ham Bone, Ham Bone, where'd you stay?
I met a pretty girl an' I couldn't get away.
Ham Bone, Ham Bone, what'd you do?
Hopped up to Miss Lucy doo'.
Ask Miss Lucy will she marry me.
I wouldn't care if her poppa didn't see.
Aw, Ham Bone.

"LITTLE SALLY WALKER"

Ring game songs involved clapping, rhyming, body movements, and several players. It was not unusual to find young girls actively involved in "Little Sally Walker." One girl stood in the middle of a circle of girls. Then she would put her hands on her hips and sassily shake her body toward the one she chose to be the next one in the middle.

Little Sally Walker
Sitting in a saucer
Rise, Sally, Rise
Wipe your weeping eyes
You put your hand on your hip
And let your backbone slip
Aah, shake it to the east,
Aah, shake it to the west,
Oh, shake it to the one that you love the best!

"MR. RABBIT"

A favorite fable character was Bruh Rabbit, a clever animal who could outwit the bigger, stronger Mr. Wolf. Bruh or "Mister" Rabbit was beloved by my people. He could ease in and out of tough situations, and was basically defenseless and mild. However, the rabbit could be vain and egotistical, and when he was, he often found himself in trouble. His life taught a lesson: Be cunning when dealing with the slavemaster — perhaps depicted in the character of Mr. Wolf — but be humble when dealing with friends. In this tale, Mr. Rabbit is seen as an innocent creature, somewhat pleased with himself, but careful not to be boastful.

Mr. Rabbit, Mr. Rabbit,
Your ears are mighty long.
Yes, kind sir,
They're put on wrong!
Every little soul must shine, shine, shi-ine,
Every little soul must shine, shine, shine.

Mr. Rabbit, Mr. Rabbit,
Your coat's mighty gray.
Yes, kind sir,
'Twas made that way!
Every little soul must shine, shine, shi-ine,
Every little soul must shine, shine, shine.

Mr. Rabbit, Mr. Rabbit,
Your feet mighty red.
Yes, kind sir,
I'm almost dead!
Every little soul must shine, shine, shi-ine,
Every little soul must shine, shine, shine.

Mr. Rabbit, Mr. Rabbit,
Your tail's mighty white.
Yes, kind sir,
I'm gettin' out o' sight!
Every little soul must shine, shine, shi-ine,
Every little soul must shine, shine, shine.

And Before I'll Be a Slave:

SONGS *of* REBELLION *and* FREEDOM

AT ALL COSTS (TOP)
A group of teenaged slaves fight off would-be captors in Loudon County, Virginia, in this engraving from William Still's book The Underground Railroad, *published in the late nineteenth century.*

STAYING TOGETHER (BELOW)
Though rare, occasionally whole families of slaves would escape together, as evidenced by this 1847 reward poster.

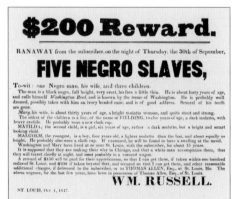

AT WHAT POINT did a person decide that death was preferable to slavery? Did he or she ponder the idea for months or years, or arise one morning vowing to be free? Some say the desire came after years of toil, others say after family was sold, some say after one too many beatings. However and whenever it came, it was a life-changing decision. Once a slave chose freedom—at any cost—he could never be enslaved again.

My people signaled their discontent. One could hear it in their songs. They echoed throughout the fields where, with backs bent, fingers aching, and dreams fading, slaves planted rice, picked cotton, and hacked sugar cane to enrich their masters. Their voices rose as they returned to their cabins after twelve hours of slave labor. "Members don't get weary, Members don't get weary, Members don't get weary," they sang to encourage one another, "For the work's almost done." Their spirituals told of the enslaved's longing to be free. Their songs sent a message, filled with symbolism and metaphors, telling how and when and why they would flee. When the enslaved sang of David, Joshua, and Moses, they were singing of liberators—members of the Underground Railroad who would lead them out of bondage. When they sang of chariots, wheels, travel shoes, and ships, they were singing of modes of transportation and escape. For my people, Canaan, Heaven, Zion, and Paradise were not just Biblical concepts, but code names for the free states, Canada, and Liberia. When slaves sang of the Jordan River, they were speaking of the Ohio River and the Atlantic Ocean. If one crossed either, he or she would know freedom.

Some spirituals plainly told of my people's intent. "Go Down, Moses" warned "Pharaoh," the slaveholder, to "let my people go." "Steal Away" told of one's intent to flee. "Oh Freedom" made it clear that one preferred death over slavery. Slaveholders forbade my people's singing these songs; those who disobeyed faced punishment.

TAKING FLIGHT
A family of fugitive slaves crosses the Rappahannock River in the early 1860s.

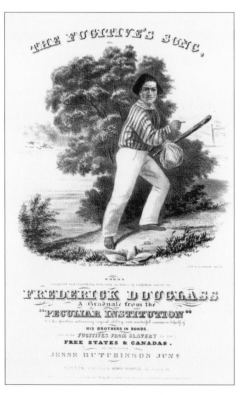

FREEDOM FIGHTER (BELOW)
*This cover of a popular aboli-
tionist songbook was dedicated
to Frederick Douglass.*

My people's folklore tells of Africans brought to this country who refused to be enslaved. Some chose death, some simply "flew away." They speak of the Ibo landing on St. Simons Island, Georgia. There, enslaved Africans longing for freedom and home agreed to take their own lives. They linked arms, waded deep into the Dunbar River, saying, "Water brung us and water take us back home." According to legend, that's where the song "Oh Freedom" was born, sung in honor of the Ibo who chose death over bondage. Another story survived, of people who could fly — Africans with magical powers. With the aid of a conjurer, the enslaved dusted themselves with a mystical powder and chanted powerful words. Magically they sprouted wings, turned into huge black birds, and flew to Africa where they were again free. Whether these Africans physically flew, no one can say. But in the slave states of Delaware, Maryland, Virginia, and North Carolina, one could hear my people sing, "I turned my eyes towards the sky, sky, and ask de Lord, Lord for wings to fly." Surely they longed to join their fellow Africans who took to the air for freedom.

The enslaved did not have to rely on folklore alone to hear tales of escape or defiance. It seemed everyone knew of one who could not be broken. There were stories of those who fled, stood up to the overseer, lived in the woods, and even made it to the North. My people spoke of them in hushed tones. These men and women became legends. A former slave from Tennessee spoke proudly of his father: "He was as mean as a bear. He was so bad to fight and so trouble-some he was sold four times to my knowing and maybe a heap more times." [29] Another told of his grandfather who roamed at will: "He could outrun bloodhounds, till they were too tired to jump over the fence…. Four patterols died owing him a whipping." [30] Still another former slave bragged that no man ever beat his mother, she was so tough that "no man ever down her." If the enslaved needed heroes, they did not have to look far. Freedom fighters were always in their midst.

What folklore and oral history didn't capture, this nation's newspapers and historians did. Harriet Tubman, a leader of the Underground Railroad, wouldn't be a slave. She brought more than 300 people out of bondage. She never was caught, never lost a passenger, never allowed any-one to turn back. Determined and courageous, Harriet believed she had two choices in life. "I had reasoned dis out in my mind; there was one of two things I had a right to, liberty or death; if I could not have one, I would have de oder; for no man should take me alive; I should fight for my liberty as long as my strength lasted, an' when de time came for me to go, de Lord would let dem take me." [31] As she made her initial escape she passed the cabin doors of her family and friends. Lifting her voice in song, she let them know of her intentions: "I'll meet you in de mornin', When you reach de promised land. On de oder side of Jordan, For I'm boun' for de promised land." On returning to free others ready to escape, she would walk in the woods, past their dwellings, and sing "Wade in the Water," telling fugitives how to throw bloodhounds off their trail. She assured them that "God's gonna trouble [stir] the water," as He did the pool of Bethesda in the Gospel of John, transforming it into healing waters — a route by which they could escape.

Nat Turner, a slave preacher, boldly defied the slave system. His revolt in Southampton, Virginia, in 1831 ended in death for more than sixty whites before he was hung. News of his revolt traveled throughout the slaveholding states. His decision to revolt was spurred by a vision. Turner stated he saw "white spirits and black spirits engaged in battle, and the sun was darkened — the thunder rolled in the Heavens and blood flowed in streams—and I heard a voice saying, 'Such is your luck, such you are called to see, and let it come rough or smooth, you must surely bear it.' " [32] Turner answered his calling. He recruited members, who petitioned others by singing, "O join 'em all, Join for Jesus, Join the Jerusalem band." To call a meeting among his followers, Turner's voice would ring out, "Let us break bread together on our knees. When I fall on my knees with my face to the rising sun, oh Lord have mercy on me." Today, "Let Us Break Bread Together" is sung in the Protestant church as a communion hymn. Some credit the song's origin to Nat Turner, who used it to call secret gatherings to plan his revolt.

For Margaret Garner, who faced re-enslavement, death was the preferred choice. She fled Kentucky with her four children, crossing the Ohio River to freedom. When captured by slave hunters, she killed two of her children, the others taken from her before she could deal them the same "merciful" blow. Margaret drowned herself as slave catchers forced her and her family back across the Ohio River. She only wished she could have taken her other two children to the water's depth with her. One can almost hear her welcoming death: "Oh when I come to die, Oh when I come to die, Oh when I come to die, Give me Jesus. Dark midnight was my cry, Dark midnight was my cry, Dark midnight was my cry, Give me Jesus. In the morning when I rise, In the morning when I rise, In the morning when I rise, Give me Jesus."

Eleven-year-old Henry of Upson County, Georgia, was tired of being a slave. In a heat of rage he slew the slaveholder's son—a child near his age who had taunted him and threatened to have him whipped. Henry was tried and hung for murder. He died young, but in death he was free. The town was shocked at the crime. Henry was "as good a slave as any," they commented. They couldn't fathom why Henry had killed; they didn't understand his burning desire for freedom. Perhaps in his last days, the youth looked at his mother and assured her, "I am not afraid to die, I am not afraid to die, I am not afraid to die, Jesus rides the milk-white horse, I am not afraid to die. Satan rides the iron gray, Satan rides the iron gray, I am not afraid to die. I am bound for the Promised Land, I am bound for the Promised Land, I am not afraid to die."

From the first Africans brought to these shores to the last harnessed under slavery, my people wanted to be free. Some would challenge the overseer squarely; others would look death straight in the eye. When a slave grew weary of the selling, the whippings, the lack of food, and the humiliation, those suffering with him understood. When one who had enough of bending and bowing and of "no massa, yes massa, and please massa" was ready to flee—even die for freedom—my people honored his choice. The rebel found he was not alone, and though others could not or would not go with him, they joined him in spirit and in song, singing: "Oh freedom over me. And before I'll be a slave, I'll be buried in my grave and go home to my Lord and be free."

"SWING LOW, SWEET CHARIOT"

One of the more well-known spirituals, "Swing Low, Sweet Chariot" tells of escape in religious terms. Chariots, angels, the Jordan River are all religious symbols as well as symbols of freedom. The chariot speaks of movement; angels are people who aid runaways; the Jordan River is the Ohio River or the Atlantic Ocean—any body of water that would carry them to free states, Canada, or Africa.

Swing low, sweet chariot,
Coming for to carry me home.
Swing low, sweet chariot,
Coming for to carry me home.

I looked over Jordan and what did I see,
Coming for to carry me home.
A band of angels, coming after me,
Coming for to carry me home.

Swing low, sweet chariot,
Coming for to carry me home.
Swing low, sweet chariot,
Coming for to carry me home.

If you get there before I do,
Coming for to carry me home.
Tell all my friends I'm coming too,
Coming for to carry me home.

Swing low, sweet chariot,
Coming for to carry me home.
Swing low, sweet chariot,
Coming for to carry me home,
Coming for to carry me home.

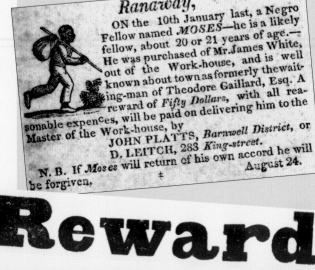

Ranaway, ON the 10th January last, a Negro Fellow named *MOSES*—he is a likely fellow, about 20 or 21 years of age.—He was purchased of Mr. James White, out of the Work-house, and is well known about town as formerly the waiting-man of Theodore Gaillard, Esq. A reward of *Fifty Dollars*, with all reasonable expences, will be paid on delivering him to the Master of the Work-house, by JOHN PLATTS, *Barnwell District*, or D. LEITCH, 283 *King-street*. N. B. If *Moses* will return of his own accord he will be forgiven. August 24.

Reward.

WITH PRIDE (TOP)
Black soldiers fight at the battle of Milliken's Bend in a drawing circa 1861-1865.

MAN IN UNIFORM (BELOW)
Hubbard Pryor, an escaped slave, joined the Forty-Fourth Colored Infantry.

John Brown's Body: SONGS *of* OUR SOLDIERS

THEY STOOD TALL, black soldiers in the Union blue. They were free men, former slaves and runaways, illiterate and learned, mulatto and jet black. They had heard of the war, the big gun shoot, of Yankees who would free them. They may not have been sure if the North would win, but if the war was lost, it would not be because black men were unable or unwilling to fight. They looked to the day when President Lincoln would stand victorious and Jefferson Davis, president of the Confederacy, would stand bowed in shame and defeat. But more than anything, they looked to the day when all black people could be free.

Nearly 180,000 black men fought on the Union side, serving proudly in the United States Colored Troops. It was with pride that black soldiers sang, "Don't you see the lightning? Don't you hear the thunder? It isn't the lightning, It isn't the thunder, It's the buttons on the Negro uniforms!"

But a black soldier's life was not easy. They found they were battling on two fronts. They battled the racism and skepticism of the U.S. War Department that felt black men would not make good soldiers, and against the bayonets and bullets of the angry South that would rather kill a black soldier than take him captive. Although black men enlisted to fight, they were used for fatigue duty first, as soldiers second. They faced prejudice, loneliness, ill treatment, and low or no pay. They dug ditches, loaded and unloaded supplies, cleaned, cooked, and buried the dead. No doubt, as they stood waist deep in stinking trenches, frustrated with their lack of training, they sang "Do You Think I'd Make Soldier?" believing full well that they would.

Still they strove to make their country proud. It was as though it was a disgrace to give up or give in. Even when the government doubted the black soldier's worth, he held fast to his duty, to prove the doubters wrong. Perhaps to encourage themselves in the face of doubt, black soldiers sang, "I can't stay behind, my Lord, I can't stay behind, Dere's room enough, room enough, Room enough in de heaven for de sojer, Can't stay behind."

It was here, around fires in front of lonely tents, in the army camps, on the blood-soaked battlefields, that black men, strong brave soldiers, sang of love and family and home. They sang of death too, knowing it was always near, and of living the Christian life so when they died they would be ready to meet their God. While battle was honorable, each man longed for freedom and peace and to be reunited with the ones he left behind. R. C. Smith, a former slave from Oklahoma, remembered hearing black soldiers sing: "If I had a drink of brandy, No longer would I roam, I'd drink it wid dat gal of mine, Dat wishes me back home."[33]

Colonel Thomas Wentworth Higginson, the white commander of the First South Carolina Volunteers, wrote often in his diary of the songs of black soldiers and their music. "Give these people their tongues, their feet and their leisure and they are happy," marveled Higginson. "At every twilight the air is full of singing, talking, and clapping of hands in unison."[34]

They sang boldly of victory, recalling Moses at the Red Sea. "My army cross over, My army cross over, O' Pharaoh's army drownded, My army cross over." They encouraged the soldier to carry on. "One more valiant soldier here, To help me bear de cross."

And they sang of death and the peace it brings. "I know the moonrise, I know the star-rise, Lay dis body down. I walk in the moonlight, I walk in de starlight, To lay dis body down. I'll walk in the graveyard, I'll walk through the graveyard, To lay dis body down. I'll lie in de grave and stretch out my arms, Lay dis body down."

As the war progressed, black soldiers did see battle, fought valiantly, and died for freedom. Their heroics were praised at the battles of Port Hudson, Milliken's Bend, Fort Wagner, and Petersburg. They fought to the death, suffering heavily in battles that many felt were ill-fated. But they stood their ground and held the flag high. Surely there was one, wiping away his tears as he held his dying comrade, who quietly sang, "We will fight for liberty, Till de Lord shall call us home; We'll soon be free, Till de Lord shall call us home."

As the war ended, as the Southern strongholds of Richmond, Petersburg, and Charleston fell, black soldiers marched in and secured the cities. The sight of black men in uniform, carrying guns, representing the power of the nation over the evils of slavery, was one few slaves forgot. Black men, women, and children greeted this with praise, blessings, and shouts of joy. An old woman rushed with arms wide open to hug a black soldier riding on a mule. Unable to reach him she hugged the mule, shouting, "Thank God."[35] Another broke out in song, "Ye's long been a-comin', For to take de land."

In strong voices, black soldiers sang the last verse of "John Brown's Body": "Now has come the glorious jubilee, When all mankind are free."

"JOHN BROWN'S BODY"

Regarded by some as a madman, a visionary and a genius by others, white abolitionist John Brown has gone down in history as a martyr in the crusade against slavery. On October 16, 1859, Brown and a band of 21 men attacked the federal arsenal at Harper's Ferry, Virginia. The band hoped to seize enough ammunition to attack Virginia slaveholders, forcing them to free their slaves. The local and federal militia were quickly alerted, capturing Brown and his men. Although Brown's plan to free my people failed, his valiant efforts were remembered and heralded in song. Black soldiers marched while singing to the tune of "The Battle Hymn of the Republic," changing the words to honor Brown, who was hung for treason, and his fallen comrades, several of whom were black.

John Brown's body lies a-molding in the grave,
John Brown's body lies a-molding in the grave,
John Brown's body lies a-molding in the grave,
But his soul's marching on.

He captured Harper's Ferry with his nineteen
*   men so true,*
And he frightened old Virginia 'til she trembled
*   through and through,*
They hung him for a traitor, themselves the
*   traitor crew,*
But his soul's marching on.

CHORUS:
Glory, glory Hallelujah,
Glory, glory Hallelujah,
Glory, glory Hallelujah,
His soul's marching on.

John Brown died that the slave might be free,
John Brown died that the slave might be free,
John Brown died that the slave might be free,
But his soul's marching on.

Now has come the glorious jubilee,
Now has come the glorious jubilee,
Now has come the glorious jubilee,
When all mankind are free.

CHORUS (REPEATS TWO TIMES)

FREE AT LAST (TOP)
This portrait, drawn at the close of the war, celebrates the end of slavery in America. In the center is a former slave family enjoying a peaceful normal life; surrounding them are images of the hardships they once endured.

32

The Day of Jubilee: SONGS *of* EMANCIPATION

A NEW SONG (BELOW)
After the war, the newly freed slaves' traditional music and song took on a new, more joyful expression.

THE NEWS OF FREEDOM came at different times and in different ways. Some slaves heard the news January 1, 1863—the day President Abraham Lincoln signed the Emancipation Proclamation. Most learned it from Union soldiers—black and white—as they brought the news of General Robert E. Lee's surrender at Appomattox, Virginia. Some of my people heard it from the slaveholder as he finally accepted Confederate defeat. However the word came, rejoicing filled the air in the slave quarters. "No more auction block for me, No more, no more, No more auction block for me, Many thousands gone."

My people had always hovered closely around news of the war. They listened intently as master and mistress talked about the Yankees—"devils," they called them, men with tails who would eat a Negro if they ever caught one. They heard the master brag of going off to beat the Yankees and being back home before nightfall. Southern white youth taunted their slaves with songs that predicted a quick Union defeat, depicting Confederate president Jefferson Davis as the winner. Susan Snow, a slave in Mississippi, recalled white children singing. "Jeff Davis, long an' slim, Whupped old Abe wid a hick'ry limb. Jeff Davis is a wise man, Lincoln is a fool, Jeff Davis rides a gray, an' Lincoln rides a mule." To which Susan responded, "Old Gen'l Pope had a shot gun, Filled it full o' gum, Killed 'em as dey come. Called a Union band, Made de Rebels un'erstan', To leave de lan', Submit to Abraham." [36]

Slaves prayed for the Union and for President Lincoln's soldiers. "Oh Fader Abraham, Go down into Dixie's land, Tell Jeff Davis, To let my people go." They had confidence that God would see them through. "I know my Lord is a man of war, He fought my battle at Hell's dark door. Satan thought he had me fast, I broke his chain and got free at last."

Booker T. Washington recalled that during the last days of the war, there was more singing in the slave quarters than usual. They no longer disguised the meaning of freedom as life in the hereafter. "[T]hey had sung those same verses before, but they had been careful to explain that 'freedom' in these songs referred to the next world…. Now they gradually threw off the mask, and were not afraid to let it be known that 'freedom' in these songs meant freedom of the body in this world." [37]

Susie Melton of Virginia remembers freedom day clearly. She learned of it from one who heard a Yankee soldier say that President Lincoln had freed the slaves. "Ole Missus say de warn't nothin' to it! Den a Yankee soldier tole someone in Williamsburg dat Marse Lincun don signed de 'Mancipation." [38] She recalled how black men and women danced all night. As they walked in freedom they sang, "Sun, you be here an' I'll be gone. Sun, you be here an' I'll be gone. Sun, you be here an' I'll be gone. Bye, bye, don't grieve arter me, Won't give you my place, not fo' your'n. Bye, bye, don't grieve arter me, 'Cause you be here an' I'll be gone."

Freed slaves began to imagine their new lives. There would be no more rising before dawn, no more working for someone else. Fanny Berry told, "Glory, glory, yes, child. The Negroes are free, an' when they knew dat dey were free — dey — oh baby — began to sing: 'Mammy don't yo' cook no mo', Yo' ar' free, yo' ar' free. Rooster don't yo' crow no mo', Yo' ar' free, yo' ar' free. Ol' hen don't yo' lay no mo' eggs, Yo' free, Yo' free.' Sech rejoicing and shoutin' you never he'rd in your life." [39]

Georgianna Preston remembered: "Ole folks was shoutin' an' singin' songs. Dar's one dey sung purty nigh all night. Don't know who started it, but soon dey stopped, 'nother one took it up an' made up some mo' verses. Lawdy, chile, I kin hear dat song a-ringin' in my haid now: 'Ain't no mo' blowin' dat fo' day horn, Will sing, chillun, will sing. Ain't no mo' crackin' dat whip over John, Will sing, chillun, will sing.' " [40]

In the midst of their dancing, hugging, and singing, my people remembered the spirituals that had carried them through. God had promised to free them, and He had. He had promised to defeat the enemy, and He did. In their victory, my people rejoiced. "The chariot rode on the mountaintop, My God, He spoke and the chariot stopped. This is the day of jubilee, The Lord has set His people free."

Many of my people left the plantation. They walked away to start lives of their own. They looked for loved ones, found jobs in town. Many with nowhere to go stayed on the plantation, working for shares of the crops they planted or a few dollars for their skilled labor. Freedom wasn't perfect, but it was better than anything they had known. They sang in remembrance of how far they had come. "Slavery's chain done broke at last, broke at last, broke at last. Slavery's chain done broke at last, Going to praise God 'till I die."

"DOWN BY THE RIVERSIDE"

This song of jubilation expressed my people's happiness upon learning they were free. They could lay down their burdens and fears, and "study war"—the struggle to obtain freedom—no more. They could put on new clothes— symbols of a new life. They would rest on the banks of the river. They turned to the Bible, to Isaiah 2:4. "He will wield authority over the nations and adjudicate between many peoples; these will hammer swords into plowshares, their spears into sickles. Nations will not lift sword against nation, there will be no more training for war."

Gonna lay down my burden,
Down by the riverside, down by the riverside,
    down by the riverside.
I'm gonna lay down my burden, down by the riverside,
Study war no more!

CHORUS:
I ain't gonna study war no more,
    I ain't gonna study war no more,
I ain't gonna study war no more!
I ain't gonna study war no more,
    I ain't gonna study war no more,
Study war no more!

Gonna lay down my sword and shield,
Down by the riverside, down by the riverside,
    down by the riverside.
Gonna lay down my sword and shield,
    down by the riverside,
Study war no more!

CHORUS

Gonna put on my long white robe,
Down by the riverside, down by the
    riverside, down by the riverside.
Gonna put on my long white robe,
    down by the riverside,
Study war no more!

CHORUS

I'm gonna put on my starry crown,
Down by the riverside, down by the riverside,
    down by the riverside.
I'm gonna put on my starry crown,
    down by the riverside,
Study war no more!

CHORUS (REPEATS THREE TIMES)

From Plantation to Palace:

PRESERVING OUR SONGS

HUMBLE BEGINNINGS (TOP)
In 1866 Fisk University in Nashville, Tennessee was housed in nothing but a collection of former army hospital barracks.

PASS IT ON (BELOW)
Former slaves, such as this man photographed circa 1905, continued to make music an important part of their lives and in turn passed it on to the next generation.

SOME SAID IT WAS inevitable, freedpeople and the children of former slaves wanting a new song. My people had sung of slavery for 300 years. They sang of Heaven and hard times, of crossing over, of the sale, of freedom. And now, thank God, they were done. Freedpeople wanted to forget slavery, build new lives, experience the promises of freedom. Couldn't they sing with conviction, "You got a Right, I got a Right to the Tree of Life, We all got a Right to the Tree of Life"?

One could see the changes in the black community with the coming of freedom. Northern missionaries and teachers brought the former slave new songs. Black children who had yet to experience real freedom were taught "America," "Rally Round the Flag, Boys," and "The Star-Spangled Banner," often to the exclusion of Negro spirituals, ring songs, and work tunes.

Music in the black church was also changing. Troubled by white missionaries imposing stiffness on black congregations, an old woman testified: "I go to some churches and I see the folks sitting quiet and still like they don't know what the Holy Spirit is…Not make a noise! Why we make a noise about everything else…I don't want such a religion as that. I want to go to heaven the good ole way." [41]

Her heartfelt remarks touched the black worshippers. No sooner had she taken her seat than the congregation struck up an old song. "Oh, de way ter Heaben is a good ole way. Oh de way ter Heben is a right old way. Oh! De good ole way is de right ole way. Oh! I wants ter go ter Heaben in de good ole way." [42]

More so than any other group, the Jubilee Singers of Fisk University kept the Negro spirituals alive. Established in 1866 in Nashville, Tennessee, by the American Missionary Association, Fisk University was charged with providing freedmen with an education. From the beginning Fisk operated on limited funds. The buildings were once hospital barracks erected by the Union army. The officers' quarters became the homes of teachers. The sick ward was transformed into schoolrooms.

Founders and students scraped together money, but it wasn't enough. In 1871 schoolmaster George L. White decided to tour his black students to raise funds for the school. The students sang classical European music, to a lukewarm reception from audiences. Gradually, White added spirituals and plantation songs. From the hearts and experiences of former slaves rose the sorrowful songs of slavery—music that touched the souls and consciences of people everywhere. The Jubilee Singers performed before former abolitionists, curious onlookers, members of Congress, and President Ulysses S. Grant. Looking back on the tour, John Wesley Work, a teacher at Fisk, wrote: "The music made men rejoice, it made them weep, it made them ashamed, it made them better." [43] The students would have their share of hard times. They would be denied lodging from hotels that did not serve blacks; at times, meager donations would fail to cover their expenses. Yet they persevered. At the end of their first year on tour, the Jubilee Singers had raised $20,000.

Over the next few years, the Jubilee Singers would win international acclaim. They sang in concert before Queen Victoria of England and the Duke and Duchess of Argyll. The queen wept upon hearing them sing a haunting freedom song. "Steal away, steal away, steal away to Jesus, Steal away, steal away home, I ain't got long to stay here."

They received standing ovations for "Go Down, Moses" and "John Brown's Body" from commonpeople and nobility alike. They performed in the palace before the Crown Prince and Princess of Berlin. There they sang the songs of their fathers, "I've Been Redeem" and "Nobody Knows the Trouble I See." They appeared in Geneva, Switzerland, before an impressive crowd. When asked how they could enjoy songs in a foreign language, patrons replied, "We cannot understand them, but we can *feel* them." [44] By the end of their international tour in 1878, the singers had raised $150,000 for their beloved school.

There were others who worked to preserve my people's music: Ella Sheppard Moore, a former slave and pianist for the Jubilee Singers; Professor Adam Spence, Fisk University, who taught generations of students to respect the Negro spirituals; Frederick J. Work, who collected, harmonized, and published plantation songs; and Harry T. Burleigh, singer, arranger, and composer. Whites who heard and recognized the value of spirituals included Dr. Henry E. Kriehbel, who published Afro-American folk songs; and Colonel Thomas Wentworth Higginson, who recorded the words of the First South Carolina Volunteers, the first slave regiment in the Civil War. In 1867, the first anthology of slave songs, entitled *Slave Songs of the United States*, was edited by William Francis Allen, Charles Pickard Ware, and Lucy McKim Garrison. James Weldon Johnson published *The Book of American Negro Spirituals* in 1925.

Yet if one were to credit anyone with keeping spirituals alive, it was undoubtedly the former slaves. They sang spirituals under slavery to keep their spirits hopeful, they sang them under freedom as reminders of how God had brought them through. The songs the Fisk Jubilee Singers sang, that others noted, analyzed, and scored, were the songs of my people. From rugged benches in old country churches to polished oak pews of more refined gothic dwellings, elders sang, "Sometimes I'm as tossed and driven, Lord, Sometimes I don't know where to roam, But I've heard of a city called 'Heaven,' I've started to make it my home." These were true expressions of a people's suffering and faith—songs the spirit would not let die.

35

"FARE YE WELL"

"Fare Ye Well" was one of the songs sung by the Jubilee Singers. A spirited, up-beat song, it shows how students mastered complex songs with moving parts and several voices. "Fare Ye Well" told of the coming judgment of the Lord. It also told in secret of the great day when slaves would slip off to freedom, bidding, "Fare ye well!"

I'm gonna tell you about the coming of the Savior,
   Fare ye well, Fare ye well.
I'm gonna tell you about the coming of the Savior,
   Fare ye well, Fare ye well.

There's a better day a-coming, Fare ye well, fare ye well.
When my Lord speaks to his Father,
   Fare ye well, fare ye well.
Say, Father I'm tired of bearing,
   Fare ye well, fare ye well.
Tired of bearing for poor sinners,
   Fare ye well, fare ye well.

Oh preacher, fold your Bible, Fare ye well, fare ye well.
Prayer-makers pray no more, Fare ye well, fare ye well.
For the last soul's been converted,
   Fare ye well, Fare ye well.
For the last soul's been converted,
   Fare ye well, Fare ye well.

In that great gettin'-up morning,
   Fare ye well, fare ye well!
(REPEATS FOUR TIMES)

ACKNOWLEDGEMENTS

I AM MOST GRATEFUL TO Dr. David Morrow, Assistant Professor and Director of the Glee Club at Morehouse College. His thorough knowledge, musical genius, and engaging personality helped to make this book and CD possible. Dr. Morrow, I can never say "thank you" enough! My sincere thanks to the Morehouse College Glee Club, the Wendell P. Whalum Community Choir, and The Shrine of the Black Madonna Nationaires and nursery. They joyously gave of their time and their talent, bringing magic, breath, and life to every note, every Spiritual sung. A warm hug to Brazz and Tracy Evans of B. Music Studios. They opened their home and their recording studio to me and thirty other singers, sticking with the project until it was done. All my love goes to my husband, Milton "Ahdwele" Fann, for his patience and understanding. You are truly my complement, my better half. To the staff at becker&mayer!, as always, you are a joy to work with. *No Man Can Hinder Me* was your vision. Thank you for making this book and CD a reality!

— *Velma Maia Thomas*

FOOTNOTES

REMEMBER ME: SONGS OF AFRICA

1   Dena J. Epstein, *Sinful Tunes and Spirituals: Black Folk Music to the Civil War* (Champaign: University of Illinois Press, 1977), 6.

2   John Blassingame, *The Slave Community* (New York: Oxford University Press, 1972), 19.

3   Blassingame, *The Slave Community*, 20.

THE MIDDLE PASSAGE: SONGS THAT CARRIED US OVER

4   Daniel P. Mannix with Malcolm Cowley, *Black Cargoes: A History of the Atlanta Slave Trade, 1518–1865* (New York: Viking Press, 1962), 118.

5   Michael Gomez, *Exchanging Our Country Marks: The Transformation of African Identities in the Colonial and Antebellum South* (Chapel Hill: University of North Carolina Press, 1998), 200.

6   Gomez, *Exchanging Our Country Marks*, 164.

7   Mannix, *Black Cargoes*, 114.

8   James Pope-Hennessy, *Sins of the Fathers: A Study of the Atlantic Slave Trade* (New York: Knopf, 1968), 4.

9   Mannix, *Black Cargoes*, 150-151.

LORD, HOW COME ME HERE?:
HOLDING ON TO SONGS OF OUR AFRICAN PAST

10   Miles Mark Fisher, *Negro Slave Songs in the United States* (Secaucus: Citadel Press, third printing, 1978), 41.

WHEN THE HAMMER RINGS: SONGS OF WORK

11   Harold Courlander, *Negro Folk Music, U.S.A.* (New York: Columbia University Press, 1970), 91.

12   Charles Joyner, *Remember Me: Slave Life in Coastal Georgia* (Atlanta: Georgia Humanities Council, 1989), 11.

13   James Mellon, *Bullwhip Days: The Slaves Remember, An Oral History* (New York: Avon Books, 1990), 138.

14   Joyner, *Remember Me*, 11.

15   Eugene Genovese, *Roll, Jordan, Roll: The World the Slaves Made* (New York: Random House, 1976), 316.

16   Ira Berlin, *Remembering Slavery: African Americans Talk About Their Personal Experiences of Slavery and Emancipation* (New York: New Press, 1998), 177.

17   Courlander, *Negro Folk Music, U.S.A.*, 83.

THERE MUST BE A GOD SOMEWHERE:
THE BIRTH OF SPIRITUALS

18   Howard W. Odum, *The Negro and His Songs: A Study of Typical Negro Songs in the South* (Westport: Negro University Press, reprint, 1968), 18.

19   John Wesley Work, *Folk Song of the American Negro* (New York: Negro University Press, 1969), 22.

LOVE SONGS: SONGS THAT MADE OUR HEARTS SING

20   Genovese, *Roll, Jordan, Roll*, 470.

21   Berlin, *Remembering Slavery*, 126.

22   R. Emmet Kennedy, *Black Cameos* (New York: Albert & Charles Boni, 1924), 175.

LITTLE SALLY WALKER: LULLABIES AND SONGS OF PLAY

23   Frances Anne Kemble, *Journal of a Residence on a Georgian Plantation* (New York: Knopf, 1961), 130.

24   Berlin, *Remembering Slavery*, 218.

25   Lydia Parrish, *Slave Songs of the Georgia Sea Islands* (Athens: University of Georgia Press, reprint, 1992), 94.

26   Charles Perdue, Thomas E. Barden, and Robert K. Phillips, *Weevils in the Wheat: Interviews with Virginia Ex-Slaves* (Charlottesville: University Press of Virginia, 1976), 96.

27   Dorothy Scarborough, *On the Trail of Negro Folk Songs* (Cambridge: Harvard University Press, 1925), 138.

28   Wilma King, *Stolen Childhood: Slave Youth in Nineteenth-Century America* (Bloomington: Indiana University Press, 1995), 45.

AND BEFORE I'LL BE A SLAVE:
SONGS OF REBELLION AND FREEDOM

29   Genovese, *Roll, Jordan, Roll*, 626.

30   Lawrence W. Levine, *Black Culture and Black Consciousness: Afro-American Folk Thought from Slavery to Freedom* (New York: Oxford University Press, 1989), 394.

31   Sarah Bradford, *Harriet Tubman: The Moses of Her People* (New York: Corinth Books, 1961), 29.

32   Blassingame, *The Slave Community*, 128.

JOHN BROWN'S BODY: SONGS OF OUR SOLDIERS

33   Lindsay Baker, *The WPA Oklahoma Slave Narratives* (Norman: University of Oklahoma Press, 1996), 397.

34   Thomas Wentworth Higginson, *Army Life in a Black Regiment* (Boston: Beacon Press, 1962), 21.

35   Benjamin Quarles, *The Negro in the Civil War* (Boston: Little Brown and Company, 1953), 327.

THE DAY OF JUBILEE: SONGS OF EMANCIPATION

36   Berlin, *Remembering Slavery*, 216-217.

37   Albert Raboteau, *Slave Religion: The Invisible Institution in the Antebellum South* (New York: Oxford University Press, 1978), 249.

38   Perdue, *Weevils in the Wheat*, 213.

39   Perdue, *Weevils in the Wheat*, 38-39.

40   Perdue, *Weevils in the Wheat*, 233-234.

FROM PLANTATION TO PALACE: PRESERVING OUR SONGS

41   American Social History Project, *Freedom's Unfinished Revolution: An Inquiry into the Civil War and Reconstruction* (New York: New Press, 1996), 187.

42   Leon F. Litwack, *Been in the Storm So Long: The Aftermath of Slavery* (New York: Random House, 1980), 463.

43   Work, *Folk Song of the American Negro*, 111.

44   J.B.T. Marsh, *The Story of the Jubilee Singers: With Their Songs* (Boston: Houghton Osgood and Company, 1880, reprinted by AMS Press, Inc., New York, 1971), 86.

CREDITS (IMAGES)

KEY
CB: Corbis
LOC: Library of Congress
NYHS: New York Historical Society
NYPL: New York Public Library

FRONT COVER
Walter Dean Myers Collection

REMEMBER ME: SONGS OF AFRICA (PAGES 2-3)
Dancing Warriors: Hulton-Getty; Kenyan Drummer and Dancers: CB.

THE MIDDLE PASSAGE: SONGS THAT CARRIED US OVER (PAGES 4-5)
Slave Thrown Overboard (Woodcut): CB; Negroes for Sale: American Antiquarian Society; Zanzibar Slaves: CB; Slave Ships, Zanzibar Slaves, "Gold Coast Slaves" Notice, and Slavers Weighing Captive (INSIDE FLAP): CB.

LORD, HOW COME ME HERE?: HOLDING ON TO SONGS OF OUR AFRICAN PAST (PAGES 6-7)
Juba Dance: CB; Jack, Guinea Driver: Peabody Museum, Harvard; Dancing Circle: *Century* magazine (BACKGROUND); Servant Girl at Work (INSIDE FLAP): Schomburg Center, NYPL.

WHEN THE HAMMER RINGS: SONGS OF WORK (PAGES 8-11)
Cotton Field Workers: CB; Slaves in Sugarcane Field: Tulane University Archives; Slaves Transporting Cotton Bales: NYHS; Woman and Girl with Dog: LOC; Workers with Overseer: LOC.

THERE MUST BE A GOD SOMEWHERE: THE BIRTH OF SPIRITUALS (PAGES 12-13)
Three Generations: *Harper's Weekly* magazine; Spiritual Dancers: CB; Old Woman in Contemplation: LOC.

HAVE YOU GOT GOOD RELIGION?: SONGS OF BIBLICAL STORIES (PAGES 14-15)
African-American Preacher: Schomburg Center, NYPL; Prayer Meeting: CB; Man Walking Away: LOC; Congregation Under Trees (INSIDE FLAP): CB.

LOVE SONGS: SONGS THAT MADE OUR HEARTS SING (PAGES 16-19)
Wedding: CB; Jumping the Broom: Colonial Williamsburg Foundation; Couple in Front of Cabin: Valentine Museum; Painful Goodbye: CB; Women with Children: CB; Marriage Certificate (INSIDE FLAP): National Archives.

EVERYBODY SING: SONGS OF COMMUNITY (PAGES 20-21)
Slave Holiday: CB; Slaves in Front of Cabin: CB; Women and Children in Front of Home: Leib Archives; Row of Slave Quarters: NYHS; Union Contrabands (INSIDE FLAP): CB.

LITTLE SALLY WALKER: LULLABIES AND SONGS OF PLAY (PAGES 22-25)
Children Dancing: CB; Old and Young: Valentine Museum; Boys with Cart: Valentine Museum; Little Boys Standing: Valentine Museum; Banjo Player: CB.

AND BEFORE I'LL BE A SLAVE: SONGS OF FREEDOM AND REBELLION (PAGES 26-29)
Escaping Slaves Fighting Back: CB; $200 Reward: LOC; Escaped Slaves Crossing River: CB; "The Fugitive" Songbook Cover: CB; Runaway Advertisement: *Charleston Gazette*; Slaves Fleeing by Boat: Schomburg Center, NYPL.

JOHN BROWN'S BODY: SONGS OF OUR SOLDIERS (PAGES 30-31)
Battle of Milliken's Bend: CB; Hubbard Pryor: National Archives; Contrabands (BACKGROUND): CB; African-American Soldiers: NYHS.

THE DAY OF JUBILEE: SONGS OF EMANCIPATION (PAGES 32-33)
Emancipation Mural: CB; Dancing Man: CB; Newly Freed Slaves: CB; Dancing Couple: CB.

FROM PLANTATION TO PALACE: PRESERVING OUR SONGS (PAGES 34-35)
Fisk University, 1866: Fisk University Archives; Old Minstrel: Schomburg Center, NYPL; Fisk Jubilee Singers: CB.

CREDITS (CD)

All songs recorded, engineered, mixed, and mastered at B. Music Studios in Atlanta, Georgia, by Brazz P. Evans III of Fairmont, West Virginia.

B. Music Studios
P.O. Box 2020
Decatur, GA 30031
(404) 244-3766
tracylew@bellsouth.net

1. **DRUMMING**
   CONGAS BY ATIBA CAZEMBE

2. **KUM BA YA**
   VOCALS BY VELMA MAIA THOMAS
   TRADITIONAL

3. **LORD, HOW COME ME HERE?**
   VOCALS BY SERWA TUPONILE (EVELYN BETHUNE)
   INTERVIEW BETWEEN VELMA MAIA THOMAS AND SERWA TUPONILE (EVELYN BETHUNE)
   TRADITIONAL

4. **JOHN HENRY**
   LEAD VOCALS BY WILLIAM TRICE
   BACKGROUND VOCALS BY BEN FREEMAN, JR.
   TRADITIONAL

5. **BALM IN GILEAD**
   VOCALS BY VELMA MAIA THOMAS
   TRADITIONAL

6. RIDE ON KING JESUS
VOCALS BY VELMA MAIA THOMAS AND CHORUS
ARRANGED BY DAVID MORROW

7. WERE YOU THERE?
VOCALS BY VELMA MAIA THOMAS
TRADITIONAL

8. WITNESS
VOCALS BY ROSCOE BOYD AND CHORUS
ARRANGED BY DAVID MORROW

9. BABY IN A GUINEA-BLUE GOWN
VOCALS BY DAVID MORROW
ARRANGED BY DAVID MORROW

10. TRAMPIN'
VOCALS BY WILLIAM TRICE AND CHORUS
ARRANGED BY WENDELL P. WHALUM

11. HAM BONE, HAM BONE
SPOKEN INTRODUCTION BY ELLIS PHELPS
LEAD VOCALS AND HAND SLAPPING BY BRAZZ P. EVANS III
BACKGROUND VOCALS BY BEN FREEMAN, JR., BEN FREEMAN III, ANTOINE
FREEMAN, AND CHRISTOPHER FREEMAN
TRADITIONAL

12. LITTLE SALLY WALKER
VOCALS BY VELMA MAIA THOMAS
BACKGROUND VOCALS BY SHANICE ELDER AND SHERIECE ELDER
SOUND EFFECTS BY BRAZZ P. EVANS III
TRADITIONAL

13. MR. RABBIT
LEAD VOCALS BY VELMA MAIA THOMAS
BACKGROUND VOCALS BY ANDAIYE AYINDE, KINAYA AYINDE,
OBASI CHIOKE, DANIELLE "TSHAY" CLARK, TIJARA DELANEY,
OLU FANN, NAJINGA LUSTER, AYODELE MAWULI, KALIF MOMBERA,
MALACHI SORRELLS, AND AYAN TULINAGWE-TAHIMBA
YOUTH CHOIR COORDINATED BY LUTALO SANIFU
TRADITIONAL

14. WADE IN THE WATER
VOCALS BY KATHRYN STANLEY
TRADITIONAL

15. SWING LOW, SWEET CHARIOT
VOCALS BY VELMA MAIA THOMAS
TRADITIONAL

16. JOHN BROWN'S BODY
VOCALS BY RAMON BRYANT AND ROSCOE BOYD
DRUMS BY BRAZZ P. EVANS III

17. DOWN BY THE RIVERSIDE
VOCALS BY KATHRYN STANLEY, MARTIN WOODS, DAVID MORROW,
AND YOLANDA WILLIAMS
ARRANGED BY DAVID MORROW

18. FARE YE WELL
VOCALS BY MARTIN WALKER AND CHORUS
ARRANGED BY BRAZEAL W. DENNARD
PUBLISHED BY ALLIANCE MUSIC PUBLICATIONS

CHORUS
David Morrow, *Director*

Hilda Jenkins Allen, *Wendell P. Whalum Community Chorus*
Adahma Ayo, *Shrine of the Black Madonna Nationaires*
Roscoe Boyd, *Morehouse College Glee Club*
Ramon Bryant, *Morehouse College Glee Club*
Courtney Carey, *Morehouse College Glee Club*
Stephen Dean, *Wendell P. Whalum Community Chorus*
Crystal Harris, *Wendell P. Whalum Community Chorus*
Fumane Mawusi, *Shrine of the Black Madonna Nationaires*
Kwame Mboya, *Shrine of the Black Madonna Nationaires*
Deborah McCrimmon, *Wendell P. Whalum Community Chorus*
Kewan Smith, *Morehouse College Glee Club*
Kathryn Stanley, *Wendell P. Whalum Community Chorus*
Velma Maia Thomas, *Shrine of the Black Madonna Nationaires*
William Trice, *Morehouse College Glee Club*
Dorothy Turnipseed, *Wendell P. Whalum Community Chorus*
Patrick Whetstone, *Morehouse College Glee Club*
Yolanda Williams, *Wendell P. Whalum Community Chorus*
Martin Woods, *Morehouse College Glee Club*
R. Wayne Woodson, *Morehouse College Glee Club*
Metra Ishara Wright, *Shrine of the Black Madonna Nationaires*

Copyright © 2001 by Velma Maia Thomas

All rights reserved. No part of this book may be reproduced or transmitted in any form or by any means electronic or
mechanical, including photocopying, recording, or by any information storage and retrieval system, without permission
in writing from the publisher.

Published by Crown Publishers, Member of the Crown Publishing Group, New York, New York.

Random House, Inc. New York, Toronto, London, Sydney, Auckland
www.randomhouse.com

CROWN is a trademark and the Crown colophon is a registered trademark of Random House, Inc.

No Man Can Hinder Me: The Journey from Slavery to Emancipation through Song
is produced by becker&mayer!, Bellevue, Washington.
www.beckermayer.com

Edited by Marcie DiPietro
Designed by Amy Redmond
Art direction by Kristen Arold
Production management by Cindy Curren
Photo research by Gordon Karg

Printed and assembled in China

Library of Congress Cataloging-in-Publication Data

Thomas, Velma Maia.
    No man can hinder me : the journey from slavery to emancipation
through song / by Velma Maia Thomas.
        p. cm.
    ISBN 0-609-60719-7
    1. Afro-Americans—Music—History and criticism. 2. Spirituals
(Songs)—History and criticism. 3. Slavery—United States—Songs and
music—History and criticism. I. Title.
    ML3556 .T51 2001
    780'.89'96073—dc21
                    00-060293

ISBN 0-609-60719-7
10 9 8 7 6 5 4 3 2 1

First Edition